The Book of Pigericks

W. J. Ortega

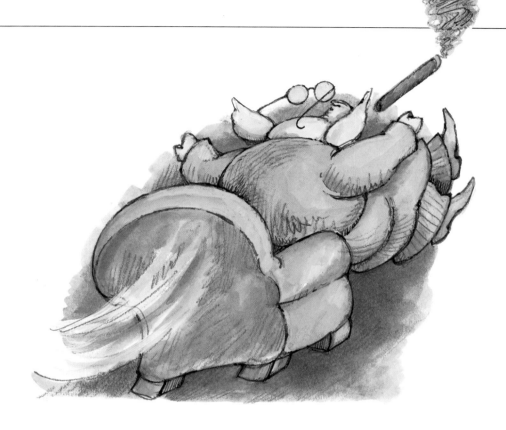

The Book of
PIGERICKS
PIG LIMERICKS
BY ARNOLD LOBEL

HarperTrophy
A Division of HarperCollins*Publishers*

Five of these pigericks previously appeared
in slightly different form in *Humpty Dumpty's Magazine*.

The Book of Pigericks
Copyright © 1983 by Arnold Lobel
Printed in the U.S.A. All rights reserved.

Library of Congress Cataloging in Publication Data

Lobel, Arnold.
The book of pigericks.

Summary: Thirty-eight original limericks
about all manner of pigs.
1. Swine—Juvenile poetry.   2. Limericks.
3. Children's poetry, American.   [1. Pigs—Poetry.
2. Limericks.   3. American poetry]   I. Title.
PS3562.018B6   1983   811'.54   82-47730
ISBN 0-06-023982-4
ISBN 0-06-023983-2 (lib. bdg.)

(A Harper Trophy book)
ISBN 0-06-443163-0 (pbk.)

First Harper Trophy edition, 1988.

To Bertram Ross and John Wallowitch

Contents

There was an old pig with a pen
Who wrote stories and verse now and then.
To enhance these creations,
He drew illustrations
With brushes, some paints and his pen.

There was a young pig whose delight
Was to follow the moths in their flight.
He entrapped them in nets,
Then admired his pets
As they danced on the ceiling at night.

There was a tough pig from Pine Bluff
Who was muscular, rowdy and rough.
At school, after classes,
The thin boys with glasses
Steered clear of that pig from Pine Bluff.

There was a sad pig with a tail
Not curly, but straight as a nail.
So he ate simply oodles
Of pretzels and noodles,
Which put a fine twist to his tail.

There was a young pig from Nantucket
Who went far out to sea in a bucket.
There she met a large fish
Who said, "Pig is my dish!"
So she sailed swiftly back to Nantucket.

There was a warm pig from Key West.

Of sandcastles, his was the best.

But as soon as he built it,

A wave came to tilt it,

Which dampened that pig from Key West.

There was a cold pig from North Stowe
Who despised winter weather and snow.
Sixteen coats never warmed him,
They only deformed him,
That frigid, cold pig from North Stowe.

There was an old pig from Van Nuys.
In the window she cooled cherry pies.
But the fruit of her labors
Was eaten by neighbors
Who came for dessert in Van Nuys.

There was a vague pig from Glens Falls
Who had lost all his windows and walls.
While in search of his floor
He misplaced his front door,
That forgetful, vague pig from Glens Falls.

There was a poor pig on the street.
In the trash he found tidbits to eat.
Though his hot garbage stew
Smelled exactly like glue,
He declared that its taste was a treat.

There was a rich pig from Palm Springs
Who had passions for bracelets and rings.
He displayed his collection
Around his midsection
By means of strong wires and strings.

There was a young pig from Schenectady

Who cried, "What is wrong with my neck today?

At ten minutes to two

It just sprouted and grew.

Now I'm taller than all of Schenectady!"

There was an old pig from South Goshen
Who awoke to a noisy commotion.
There were ten gambling mice
Playing poker and dice
On his eiderdown quilt in South Goshen.

There was a loud pig from West Wheeling
Who sang with expression and feeling.
But her voice, in its shrillness,
Could shatter the stillness
And all of the glass in West Wheeling.

There was a rude pig from Duluth
Whose manners were clearly uncouth.
For he emptied his cup
From a terrace high up,
Dropping showers of soup on Duluth.

There was a young pig from Chanute
Who could pipe little songs on a flute.
When she practiced her scales,
A large crowd of snails
Came to listen, enrapt in Chanute.

There was an old pig with a clock
Who experienced anguish and shock,
For he greased it with butter,
Which caused it to sputter
And drowned both its tick and its tock.

There was an old pig from New York

Who dined without knife, spoon or fork.

Each time he ate peas,

They rolled down to his knees—

That pea-splattered pig from New York.

There was a shy pig by a wall
Who was frightened when guests came to call.
At the sound of their chatter
His shape became flatter,
Until he was not there at all.

There was a plain pig, far from pretty,

Who was given to gloom and self-pity.

But concealing her face

Under curtains of lace,

She then merrily strolled through the city.

There was a fair pig from Cohoes
Who desired to smell like a rose.
She sprayed on some scent,
But became discontent
When a honeybee pranced on her nose.

There was a young pig who, in bed,
Nightly slumbered with eggs on his head.
When the sun at its rise
Made him open his eyes,
He enjoyed a quick breakfast in bed.

There was an old pig in a chair
Whose cigar brought his wife to despair.
With a fan she assailed,
And quite promptly exhaled
That old pig, his cigar and his chair.

There was a wet pig from Fort Wayne
Who was suddenly caught in the rain.
His suspenders and belt
Were the sort that would melt,
So his trousers were swept down the drain.

There was a small pig who wept tears
When his mother said, "I'll wash your ears."
As she poured on the soap,
He cried, "Oh, how I hope
This won't happen again for ten years!"

There was a fast pig from East Flushing.

To wherever he went, he was rushing.

So great was his speed

That his legs took the lead,

As they left him behind in East Flushing.

There was a slow pig from Decatur

Whose motto was "I'll do it later."

With the laziest slouch

He approached a soft couch,

Where he twiddled his thumbs in Decatur.

There was a stout pig from Oak Ridge
Who stepped heavily onto a bridge.
When she heard a loud *CREAK*,
She cried, "Gad, but it's weak!"
So she tiptoed the length of that bridge.

There was a light pig from Montclair.
Dressed in feathers, she floated on air.
When the birds saw her frock,
They called, "Come, join our flock!"
Which she did, in the skies of Montclair.

There was a smart pig who was able
To make use of his three-legged table.
He accomplished this trick
Standing stiff as a stick,
To be leg number four of that table.

There was a pale pig from Spokane
Who elected to lie in a pan.
There she baked in the sun
From high noon until one,
Getting very well done in Spokane.

There was a fat pig from Savannah
Who set foot on a peel of banana.
As he came crashing down,
Every person in town
Thought an earthquake was shaking Savannah.

There was a strange pig in the park

Whose behavior was odd after dark.

When the full moon appeared

He grew fangs and a beard,

Which alarmed all the folk in the park.

There was a small pig from Woonsocket
Who kept frogs and toads in his pocket.
When his dear mother scolded,
Those fellows unfolded
To jump on her hat in Woonsocket.

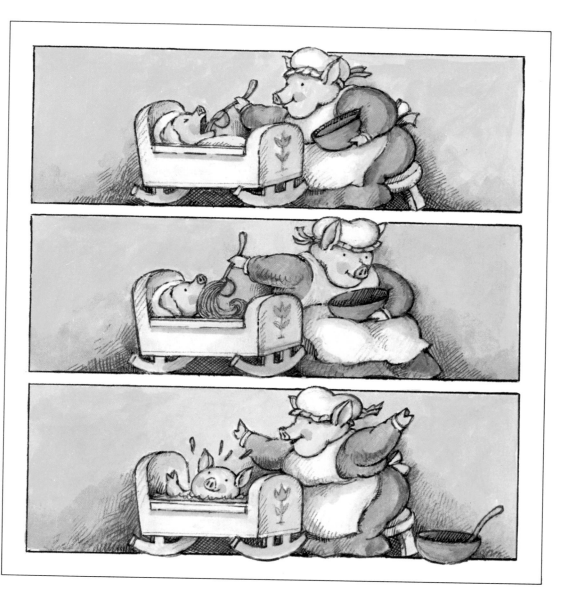

There was a young pig by a cradle
Who was feeding her babe with a ladle.
The broth reached his chin
When she spooned too much in,
So she taught him to swim in that cradle.

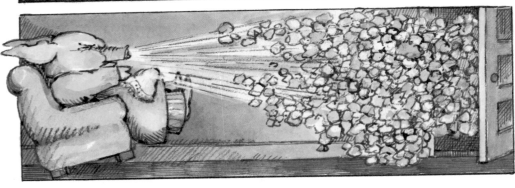

There was a sick pig with a cold

Whose discomforts could not be controlled,

For he sneezed into pieces

His two favorite nieces,

Which grieved that sick pig with a cold.

There was a young pig from Moline
Whose botanical interests were keen.
He planted his socks
In a bright window box,
And they blossomed there, flowery and green.

There was an old pig with a pen
Who had finished his work once again.
Then he quietly sat
With his comfortable cat...

While he rested his brushes and pen.